THE

HAPPY

ZONE

THE
HAPPY ZONE

Be Happier in all areas of your life...

CAREER
HEALTH & WELLNESS
FAITH
MONEY & FINANCE
RELATIONSHIPS

STEVE GEHRMANN

The Happy Zone

© 2021, Steve Gehrmann .

Print ISBN: 978-1-73707-9-002
eBook ISBN: 978-1-73707-9-019

This book is dedicated to all of the amazing happy people who let me interview them for the "Happy Zone" project, making this book possible. Without your willingness to open up to me, there would be no "Happy Zone" for others to find. Thank you so much for your support and help!

———————————————————

CONTENTS

"When I was five years old, my mother always told me that happiness was the key to life. When I went to school, they asked me what I wanted to be when I grew up. I wrote down 'happy.' They told me I didn't understand the assignment and I told them they didn't understand life."

John Lennon

Preface

Happiness is something we all seek, whether we are young or old, rich or poor, male or female.

Through interviews done in person, over the phone, via mail, email, and social media, including every age category, as well as with people who are farmers, professional athletes, doctors, financial professionals, housewives, Olympic athletes, retirees, teachers, nurses, police officers, carpenters, and business owners, the hope here is to increase your level of happiness!

The focus of the research for this book covers five areas of life: career, relationships, faith, health and wellness, and money and finances. They all go hand in hand. You master these – or at least continue to improve on them – and you master life.

Numerous studies show that happy individuals are successful in many different aspects of life, including in their careers, relationships, health, and finances. When first starting this project, I assumed that success was the key to happiness. While conducting interviews, many times people came across as very successful, yet they were not happy in their situations. Luckily, they realized this, and they were able to get out of their respective dilemmas and gain the happiness they desired.

One such gentleman worked in Silicon Valley, California. He had a big house, a new car, and just about everything he wanted. However, he was not happy. It was as if he was searching to buy happiness, but he couldn't find it. This individual wasn't doing work that excited him or that made him feel he was making a difference. He felt as if he was called to do something else. So, he left California to start a new business that is now growing, and he's happier than ever.

This story, along with many just like it, shows how being successful in others' eyes does not automatically equate to happiness. Attaining happiness is more desirable than obtaining wealth and material goods, according to many studies. It's not only obtaining happiness that promotes better well-being; it's the pursuit of it.

Dr. Robert Lustig, a professor at the University of California, San Francisco and author of *The Hacking of the American Mind* says, "The constant seeking of pleasure, whether it's from shopping, drugs, sex, or food makes it harder and harder to feel happy." This is true. One can be happy for a short while after purchasing something, but the happiness doesn't last. Enjoying the little things brings happiness. While these "little things" happen all the time, we miss a lot of them since they are not as intense as the quick impulses of other pleasures.

So, why did I write this book? I want more people to enjoy more happiness more often. If this can happen, maybe the world will be a better place.

Introduction

What is your definition of happiness? What is your definition of success? Each of us has our own definitions for these words. Here is how the dictionary defines them:

Success: the accomplishment of an aim of purpose

Happiness: a state of well-being and contentment

Well-being: the state of being comfortable, healthy, or happy

Comfortable: enjoying contentment and security

Contentment: a state of happiness and satisfaction

Satisfaction: fulfillment of one's wishes, expectations, or needs

Security: the state of being free from danger or threat

Free: not under the control or in the power of another; able to act or be done as one wishes

Act: take action; do something

Action: the fact or process of doing something, typically to achieve an aim

The definition of success requires that you first have an aim or purpose to begin. Without a purpose, there cannot be success. You have to know what you want in order to be able to go out and get it.

Similarly, for happiness, there needs to be contentment. You have to be happy with what you have. Even though you may not yet have everything you want, you have to be happy with what you have at any given time. Then, you can go after everything you want.

Well-being includes being healthy. Consider your health and what you can do to improve upon it. A little change can make a big difference. It is also important to not beat yourself up over where you are now – be content where you are as you continue to improve.

By being comfortable, it is implied that you need a level of security. Enjoy what you have, all while knowing that you have what you need.

Security means freedom. This means you are in control of your actions. You and only you are in control of what you do, and that means you control your destiny and your happiness.

Actions mean you are doing something. You are content where you are while you continue to try to improve.

As you can see from the aforementioned definitions and clarifications, happiness and success must come from inside of you. My research and interviews have shown this to be the case. It has never and will never come from the outside or from anybody else but you. You come up with your own definition of success; it says as much right in the definition: the accomplishment of an aim or purpose. It is up to you to decide your aim and your purpose.

You will never enjoy happiness without a sense of contentment, without appreciating what you already have. The definition states that contentment is a state of happiness and satisfaction. It is the fulfillment of your own wishes. So, you decide. You set up your own expectations and dreams.

The Declaration of Independence, signed on July 4, 1776, in part says:

"…We hold these truths to be self-evident, that all men are created equal, that they are endowed by their Creator with certain unalienable Rights, that among these are Life, Liberty and the pursuit of Happiness. – That to secure these rights, Governments are instituted among Men, deriving their just powers from the consent of the governed. --- that whenever any Form of Government becomes destructive of these ends, it is the Right of the People to alter or to abolish it, and to institute new Government, laying its foundation on such principles and organizing its powers in such form, as to them shall seem most likely to effect their Safety and Happiness...."

Even over two hundred years ago, the Founding Fathers knew about the pursuit of happiness. They said it is up to the people to vote the elected officials out of office and institute new government.

It is up to you to create your own happiness. You can't let somebody else determine what makes you happy. This is as true today as it was more than two hundred years ago.

"Generally speaking, the most miserable people I know are those who are obsessed with themselves; the happiest people I know are those who lose themselves in the service of others...By and large, I have come to see that if we complain about life, it is because we are thinking only of ourselves."

Gordon B. Hinckley

Career Happiness

Being happy in your work life and in your career seem to be hot topics these days, and really always have been. It seems as if every article published nowadays tells of people who are not happy where they are, while some even hate their jobs. Why is this the case? When you first said, "Yes, I accept this position" at your company, you were likely more than happy at that time. What changed? What makes people so unhappy in their positions when they were so happy in the same positions when they started?

Is it because they think they should have it better than they do? Where did this idea come from, anyway? Are they comparing themselves to others? That is one fact found during many interviews with people when questioned about career success. When they compared themselves to others, it resulted in them not being as happy as before. When they let others tell them if they were successful or not, they were not as happy with their own situations. An example of one such situation is as follows:

A person was a President/CEO and at one time a professor, but as he was starting his career, he ran into a boss who was always negative, no matter how positive this person tried to be. This person was performing at a high level in the company. However, with every meeting, his boss would only dwell on the negatives, and never talk about the good the employee was doing. Soon, this person was questioning whether or not he was actually performing well. He was letting his boss dictate his happiness. He thought about quitting, but he decided to take the high road and continue to be positive – chronically positive, as he put it.

Do you know what happened? You might have guessed it. The boss was fired. Not only was the boss really negative in his job, he wasn't very good at his job.

This story goes to show that staying positive, even in the most extreme situations, is at least one key to career happiness. You also must not let others determine what makes you successful or happy.

Remember when you were so happy to accept the position you currently have? Why were you so happy at that time? If that happiness has faded over time, look back and focus on why you were happy in the first place.

One theory that may help explain this is the "hedonic treadmill," or, as it is also known, "hedonic adaptation." This term was coined by Brickman and Campbell in their essay, "Hedonic Relativism and Planning the Good Society" (1971). According to this theory, as a person makes more money, their expectations and desires rise in tandem.

So, if it is the case that one's expectations change, must one also have to change or else be left with less happiness? And, why, just because someone is making more money, do one's expectations have to change? It may have to do with the old saying about "keeping up with the Joneses."

Here again is a case in which one sees other people telling them how to be happy. It is a recipe for disaster – a recipe that one should not want to make into reality. Career happiness starts and ends with you.

Most days at your job are probably pretty decent days. Most experiences are also likely pretty good. However, the bad stuff seems to always take center stage. Why? That tends to be what others are talking about. They talk about all of the bad stuff and you get caught up in that. It's probably the case since it's easier to talk about the negative. Why is this true?

In fact, you are simply a product of human nature, and as a result of this, bad tends to overpower good. That's right -- humans were designed to be keenly aware of negative circumstances and consequences, as thinking in this way has helped humans survive. This does not have to continue, though. There are ways in which you can combat your own human nature.

The best way is to show gratitude. Gratitude is the quality of being thankful, and the readiness to show appreciation for and to return kindness. Numerous studies have shown that gratitude not only improves the ability to connect with others, which in turn improves career happiness, but it also promotes physical health.

Showing gratitude will make a big difference in just about all aspects of life. Research, found in an article in the Journal of Social and Personal Relationships (2012), even shows that discussing positive life experiences increases well-being and overall satisfaction. (A boost of positive affect: The perks of sharing positive experiences, Aug. 9, 2012 from the Journal of Social and Personal Relationships)

In one "Happy Zone" interview, a manager discussed how she recognized her team's success and even celebrated it with them. Both the manager and her team experienced greater satisfaction at work when they took the time to do this.

Here's a story that shows how one act of kindness and gratitude can be life-changing, as told by William H. Tishler, Professor emeritus of landscape architecture at the University of Wisconsin-Madison:

Acts of kindness can change a life. It happened to me many decades ago. I grew up the youngest in a large family of lower economic means. None of my siblings were able to attend college. They just could not afford it. The day after I graduated from high school, my principal called me down to his office.

Wondering if I had done something wrong, I sheepishly complied. He asked me if I had ever thought about going to college. I hadn't. Like many boys my age, my thoughts focused more on things like hunting, fishing, cars, and, of course, girls. Then, he told me he had paid for a dorm room at the university out of his own pocket, and he wanted me to give college a try. Not wanting to disappoint him, at the end of summer I took the bus to town to enroll. After graduating, I did a stint in the Army, then graduate school at Harvard. I accepted a faculty position at UW-Madison. It resulted in my spending nearly forty delightful years there, which completely changed my life. Yes, an act of kindness can change a life. Always look for opportunities to provide for someone.

Just like the professor received help even though he wasn't looking for it, one trait that kept coming up during this research was accepting help from others. One way to do this is to accept and ask for constructive criticism. This is the process of offering valid opinions about the work of others, involving both positive and negative comments. Most of the time, people don't like to hear negative comments about themselves; however, you have to understand that the information being presented to you is meant to help you to get better, and, in turn, be in a happier place. In order to get to that happier place, you must actually seek out constructive criticism.

Do this by asking others how they have been successful, and how they manage to be happy more times than not while it seems impossible for you.

During one interview with a teacher and coach, he mentioned how he is constantly looking for ways to improve in the classroom, on the court, and at home. He is always looking to grow. He does this by asking other coaches and teachers how they are doing things. He reads books and asks a lot of questions. He'll take ideas from different people and align them with his needs and wants. He puts his own spin on everything to make it his own.

A lot of others were similar in their thoughts that it is important to get help and advice from others in order to become successful, and therefore happier, in the workplace.

Not only is it important to learn from others, but it's important to celebrate with others. Celebrate their accomplishments and milestones. A lot of times it seems like others might not want you to succeed; they only want themselves to do so. It even seems like others may not want you to be happy since they are not happy. Do you ever feel this way? It is important to keep in mind that those people who only want themselves to succeed aren't truly succeeding anyway. And, you know what? If they are, they are not happy about it since they aren't sharing others' successes. This is part of career happiness – sharing and celebrating with others. One interviewee put it this way – "I just try to 'lift others up,' and what really happens is it lifts me up."

One important aspect of learning from others is to not copy. Yes, it is always wise to use good information to your advantage, but don't copy it if you don't know the situation from which it stems. It may seem really good, but not knowing another person's situation can put you in a bad spot. Here is a story to illustrate this:

There was a man who, while in high school, had to take the SAT math test. He didn't study, but he had a friend who was really smart, so he sat behind him and copied his answers. The only problem was his friend was taking a different test, so he ended up getting all of the answers wrong. Since he didn't know his friend's situation, he made a huge mistake, which started with an error in judgment. His first semester in college he had to take a remedial math course at night as a result of not doing well on his SAT math test. It goes to show that you can't live somebody else's life; you have to live yours. He did find a silver lining to this – he met a good friend in that class. So, he ended up making the best of a situation that started poorly.

After discussing this topic with a law enforcement official, he said one thing to realize is that not everything is going to be awesome, and that about 60-70 percent will be good, while the other 30-40 percent you just have to accept and let slide. Not every hour of every day is going to be the best. Accept the fact that there will be some tough times, but the good will outweigh the bad. It's kind of like the weather – when it's good, you don't really hear or talk about it, but when it's pouring rain or there is a blizzard outside, you complain about it and only remember the bad.

Fastest Way to Failure and Unhappiness with Your Career

"You pile up enough tomorrows, and you'll find you are left with nothing but a lot of empty yesterdays."

Meredith Willson,
The Music Man, as stated by Professor Harold Hill

Sometimes knowing what not to do is just as important as knowing what to do.

Someday is not a day. Saying, "Oh, I'll do that someday" will get you just what Professor Hill says: a lot of empty yesterdays, meaning you didn't do a whole lot, and most likely did not experience a lot of happy times, either. Happy people get things done and go places with others. This is how they get ahead in life and at work. It's not to say you have to always be on the go. It's just meant to say to use your time wisely. Getting things done (that maybe you don't want to do) can lead to doing things you do want to do. Time management is a big part of being happy at work and at home. If you're rushing around like a chicken with its head cut off, it's hard to be happy. Just like the legendary UCLA coach John Wooden would tell his players: "Be quick, but don't hurry," as you can do a lot of things without being in a rush. Rushing allows us to make mistakes and end up on the wrong side of happy. When was the last time you were rushing into work while fighting traffic and you were happy? It's hard to be happy when you are running late. Start just a bit earlier and avoid the headaches.

Thinking about the "right now" is a big part of being in the "Happy Zone" as well. Being content about where you are and what you are doing, along with not worrying about the past or what may or may not happen in the future, is of vital importance. Living in the now is about concentrating on what you are doing at any given moment. Actually, "now" is a magical word that gets you to the "Happy Zone." If you concentrate on what you are doing now, it means you are not contemplating what may happen in the future or what has already happened in the past. Right now can't change the past, and if you concentrate on the right now, you set the stage for a happier tomorrow.

There are many people who may not have always enjoyed their pasts, but they simply did not worry. They learned from their pasts and made improvements in the now so the future turned out better.

Some people have a hard time letting go of the past or even not worrying about the future. Most people get over this by simply concentrating on what they are doing at present. You may have a lot to do and it may seem insurmountable; however, if you take it one step at a time, one task at a time, you will have a much better chance of accomplishing everything rather than thinking about everything all at once and becoming overwhelmed.

Ways to Improve
Your Career Happiness:

- **Stop Comparing** – There will always be somebody more successful, more accomplished, or more financially set. Making this comparison means you will likely never measure up. Have your own meaning of success and what it means to be happy based on what matters most to you, not to others.

- **Keep Improving** – Keep learning. Become an expert in your field. There's always something to learn and something to work toward achieving. Even if it's something very small, it will add up over time. Become somebody at your company whom they can't afford to lose.

- **Take Constructive Criticism** – This will be in the form of both positive and negative comments; they are not to be taken completely negatively. You should listen and learn from this as it is meant to help you grow in your career.

- **Find Out How Others Have Done It** – Find somebody in your field who is successful and happy; then, ask them how they have achieved their own success. They'll love to talk about themselves and offer you help.

- **Show Gratitude** – Be thankful for what you already have as you go after all you want, and show your appreciation toward others. Be positive with yourself and with others at the same time.

"To have an idea what genuine human compassion is like, look at children. Naturally open and honest, they don't care about other children's background, what their religion or other nationalities are, so long as they smile and play together. It's as we grow older that's when the trouble begins – we only smile to get what we want. But when we see other human beings as being like us and show concern – that's genuine compassion."

Dalai Lama

Be Happier in Your Relationships

Many people are realizing THINGS are not as important as PEOPLE. The true gift in life is the time spent with loved ones. Relationships are BIG. It turns out, too, the little things are the BIG things in life.

This is a story of a college kid, Jim, whose roommate, Brian, was a big NASCAR fan, while he himself was definitely not. Brian talked about how great it was to watch the races and how interesting they were. On the other hand, Jim had no interest in watching the cars go around and around in circles and he let Brian know how dumb he thought it was. Brian said it was much more than watching cars driving in circles. They had to make pit stops, change tires, and on and on. He didn't listen at all to the negative comments Jim was making.

Fast forward about fifteen years, and Jim, who had so disliked NASCAR years prior, now has a son who loves to watch races. What does Jim, the father, do? He watches with his son and actually enjoys it. Why? He is doing something with someone whom he loves. It doesn't make much difference what they do, as long as they do it together. The funny thing is he actually started to enjoy NASCAR and came to see the many aspects of the sport that his college roommate talked about, including pit stops and the like.

It's important in a relationship for some give and take. Even though you, at first, may not necessarily like your child's or spouse's hobbies, you can still enjoy them together. It's all about being creative. That is what counts the most.

This is one of the traits that was revealed time and time again while discussing relationships in interviews: doing things together. Many times, it wasn't something super extravagant. It was simply about doing something together, like taking a walk in the park, going to the grocery store, cooking a meal, having friends over for dinner, engaging in a simple talk after work, taking a spontaneous day trip or even a walk around the block, or maybe even watching TV together.

Speaking to couples who have been married for forty, fifty, sixty and even seventy years, there were some definite common traits revealed. If you've been together for over seventy years, you for sure know how to be happy and successful in your relationship!

One couple who has been married over seventy years stated how they share responsibilities. The husband wasn't so good with the checkbook, so the wife took care of that. The husband enjoyed cooking, so she let him cook meals for the family. They both enjoyed entertaining, so they worked together on that. They both agreed to help each other with cleaning since neither one of them enjoyed any type of cleaning, including laundry. They said it boiled down to helping each other. This same couple shared another trait that many others shared as well: the willingness to compromise, which can be summed up as: It's not all about you.

It seems easy, but in the heat of the moment, it's not always that way, so know that there will be times of disagreement. This is the time to take a step back, gather yourself, take a deep breath, and

ask if it will matter in five years. Don't fuss over the little stuff. One couple described it to me like so: "We used to get really angry with each other and then for one to two days we'd not even talk to each other, and then we'd miss each other. Sometimes you don't know what you have till it's gone, and then it may be too late."

Even though there may be a disagreement, that doesn't mean you have to have conflict. You have to be willing to let it go. Leave room for mistakes, and respect each other. You have to understand that just because you do it one way, it doesn't mean it's the only way. Give others the benefit of the doubt. Be willing to listen to both sides and find common ground. There may even be a need to apologize, say you're sorry, and explain why. Don't let things fester and grow, as it'll only make it worse.

A sales manager stated: "I am third. God, Family, then me. If it's something that is selfish, then it's probably bad." He continued to say that just being there for each other is really important. Just the fact that you are there listening, and not judging. Your time is not only important to you, but to others. It's about sharing that time with each other.

Another happy couple explained their success and happiness by sharing:

Twenty-nine years ago we became husband and wife. We could have never predicted how those twenty-nine years would go. To say it has always been easy or wonderful would not be true. Our twenty-nine years together have had ups and downs, but together we have made a wonderful life. Some days we may not like each other, but we have always loved each other. If someone says marriage is easy, they are lying to you. A real marriage goes through trials and tribulations, but together you fight for what you believe in. We believe in US!"

They went on to say

We are truly blessed after twenty-nine years. Three children who have grown into amazing adults, living their best lives, doing what they do best, in careers they all love. A wonderful daughter-in-law and son-in-law who make our son and daughter so happy. And two amazing grandsons that bring so much joy to our lives already. There is nothing better than to watch your children become parents themselves. We have been blessed. You can never, ever imagine this feeling watching them hold their little ones and seeing the instant love they have for them.

We may not have the biggest house, the fanciest cars, the highest paying jobs, the biggest savings account, but what we do have is worth so much more! I will take my time with my husband, children, their spouses, and our grandchildren over anything money can buy.

Memories spent together are priceless; you can't put a price tag on memories. Time goes way too fast! DON'T BLINK! Enjoy every minute with your loved ones, big or small, happy or mad, always tell them you love them – each and every day. Twenty-nine years have flown by.

This is a great example of a relationship that puts others first. This was a common theme among just about all interviewees. It shows how it is not all about any one person. There are other people in a relationship. The story above illustrates this perfectly. There's the husband and wife, along with the children, grandchildren, and the daughter-in-law and son-in-law. All together, they form an amazing relationship based on who they are to each other and how they spend their time together. This couple may not have had the best of everything, but they definitely made the best of everything.

Just because the relationship isn't all about you doesn't mean that it's not at least a little about you. You do have to be happy with yourself and take some time for yourself. How is this done? It's done by giving to others, sharing your life with others, working and communicating together, letting the little stuff slide, and forgiving others. When there is disagreement, walk away and ask yourself if it really matters, then take time to cool down. Take time for yourself at the beginning and end of every day. Set some goals at the start and see how the day went at the end; then see what you can improve upon for the next day. If you can improve just a little each day, your relationships will be amazing, including with yourself.

In relationships, especially with people you love, it's important to listen even when you want to talk. We're probably all guilty of this from time to time as we love to talk about ourselves and be happy with ourselves. Communication is a key component of happy relationships. Most importantly, it's the listening part that outweighs all others. Almost everyone interviewed, from young to older, mentioned listening as a source of success and happiness in their relationships.

A set of sixteen-year-old twins said that spending time together and finding common interests was how they found the most happiness and success in their relationships. On the other end of the spectrum, one husband who had been married seventy-two years put it this way: "I always agreed with the wife." He said this with a little smirk, then went on to say that what he really meant was how they were devoted to each other, and they always kept their word and helped each other.

Relationships have to do with more than just the people we know. They deal with people we don't know as well. We are all human beings and need to be treated as such. This story from a gentleman from Minneapolis illustrates that point:

> I get very uncomfortable when I'm approached by strangers asking for money. I don't have it all figured out and get pretty uncomfortable in those situations. But I'd like you to meet someone named Antonio. He said to me, 'I'm not going to lie. I need some money, but I also want to tell you that you shouldn't be down here. This is the horrible part of town. Really nothing except crime drugs and filth – you should really go.' I wouldn't have even thought about stopping, but I was on fumes and needed gas. As I pumped my gas, we started talking and he told me he had gotten out of prison recently and that he just couldn't seem to find a way out.
>
> He said he really would just like to leave the neighborhood he was in because it was so horrible. I told him if he ever got to Minneapolis, I'd get him a job interview, thinking that would probably scare him off.
>
> He actually had a tear running down his face when he said to me: 'You promise me you can give me a job interview if I go to Minneapolis?' I said, 'Antonio, I'm not going to promise things I can't deliver, and I can't let you stay at my house – I have four kids that are my priority financially, but I'm happy to direct you to Social Services and I promise you I will get you a job interview that would pay you a decent wage. I know enough people that would at least hire you, but you have to do the rest.'

I couldn't believe what he said next. He said, 'Could you please take out your phone and look up a couple phone numbers for me? I'm going to start working on this right away. I need a change of scenery and if you are really willing to help me, I won't let you down.' I guess the moral of the story is be careful what you tell people you will do for them; they might just ask you to do it. I don't know what the chances are that I'll hear from him again, but I gave him a phone number and name of someone that will interview him and I told him again that if he got to Minneapolis, I'd help him out. I keep thinking I probably should've done a little bit more. It was a bad part of town and I was happy to get out with all four tires on my car. I just kept thinking of all the people that have helped me out over and over again even after I've made grave mistakes and should not have been given any more chances. So, I would say that what I told Antonio wasn't really from me, it was from all the people that have helped me over the years.

The story is about helping others that you don't even know. It's about people helping people in times of need. It may be your loved ones, or it may be a complete stranger. This is a big part of a happy relationship with yourself and others – helping others.

I put this to the test and found out it was actually kind of exhilarating. It made me feel very happy, but it was very strange and abnormal as well. There is a phrase, 'Pay it forward,' which means responding to one person's kindness by being kind to someone else in return. Think of the gentleman from Minneapolis as he took the support he received from others and 'paid it forward' to Antonio. Sometimes you 'pay it forward' out of the kindness of your heart without any kind of prompting from others.

One day, I gave it a try. I went to McDonald's and decided I would go to the drive through to order my food and pay for the person behind me. It was kind of a strange feeling. I knew it was going to make me happy to help somebody else and all, but it also kind of felt strange, as I'd never done something like that before. It almost felt like I was afraid to do it. Like somebody might think I'm really weird for doing something like this. Why did I feel this way? Why did I care what others thought of me? I guess it's because we're all human and we want to be accepted.

I went to the first window and asked the clerk how much the next person owed and paid their bill in addition to my own. I don't know what that person did as I didn't stick around to watch, but I hope down the road they might do something similar.

I challenge you to do something like this in the near future. It may not be at a fast-food drive through, but 'pay it forward' without looking for any type of repayment. Make it yours. You come up with the idea and then do it. Don't worry about how it may be perceived by others. Just know it's the right thing to do.

Fastest Way to Failure and Unhappiness with Your Relationships

"For every minute you are angry
you lose sixty seconds of happiness."

Ralph Waldo Emerson

It's important to know what to do and what not to do in order to have success and happiness in your relationships. Anger is one of those things not to do. There will be times you get upset about things; however, that cannot be the norm. From time to time, you will be upset, but you must realize it will pass and you will have to move on. Other people may make you angry with what they do, but you have to know it's what they did, not you. You can choose to react in a different way instead of getting out-of-control angry. How you react is up to you. And most of the time when you look back at what made you so angry in the first place, it really was not that big of a deal at all. Most of the time if you just let the little stuff go, you will eliminate much of the anger and be able to move on much more quickly.

Reflection is a big part of being happy in relationships and all other parts of the 'Happy Zone.' Part of moving forward is looking back, reflecting on what happened, and improving on that the next time. It's part of making yourself better. In relationships, this means the relationship you have with yourself. If you're not happy with yourself, there's a good chance you will not be happy with others. Much of the time people get angry with themselves for what they have or have not done, and it spills into their relationships with others. If you can improve on yourself, you can improve upon your relationships with others.

If you work on making others happy in your relationships, this in itself will go a long way in making your relationship with yourself that much better. When you make others happy, you'll find that your own happiness improves. When you only try to make yourself happy is when the trouble begins. Yes, there is time for self-reflection, but this is not an all-the-time thing. When you come home from a tough day at work and you're in a bad mood, don't let it spill over to the rest of the evening. If you do get a bit upset, realize it, say you are sorry, and get back to what matters – the loved ones in your life.

Let the bad stuff stay where it is – in the past – while you enjoy what you have right now; the present with your family and friends.

Sometimes you even learn what not to do from others, like this gentleman: "I realized from my parents' lifestyle and them waiting until I turned eighteen for their divorce, that I was bound and determined that marriage was a one-time thing and it had to be the right person that had the same morals as me. I did not want to go through the same thing my parents did."

Ways to Be Happier in Your Relationships:

- **Show Gratitude** – Be thankful for the relationships you have and show appreciation and compassion toward others. Be positive with yourself and others at the same time.

- **Reflect on the Past and Move On** – Learn from any past mistakes and aim to always be better. Don't let things fester; move on.

- **It's Not All About You** – By helping others, you will actually be helping your own happiness. When it's all about you is when your own happiness declines. Listen to others and learn about them.

- **Stay Involved** – Do things together, even if it's something like a walk around the block or a picnic in the park. Stay in touch with friends and family.

- **Make Room for Mistakes** - Nobody is perfect, including you. Mistakes happen. Say you're sorry, and when somebody else is sorry, take them at their word.

Happiness cannot be traveled to, owned, earned, worn, or consumed. Happiness is the spiritual experience of living every minute with love, grace, and gratitude."

Denis Waitley

Be Happier with Your Faith

In the 2019 NFL playoffs, the kicker for the Chicago Bears had a chance to win the game in the last seconds with a 43-yard field goal. He missed the kick, and his team lost. He took full responsibility for the loss, even though football is a team game and there were many other opportunities lost in the game. After the kick, he looked to the sky to give thanks. Many athletes do this as they come on the field, after they score a touchdown, or when they make a free throw. How many times have you seen an athlete do this?

It's easy to be thankful during the good times; however, we should be thankful at all times. We only get one chance in life before we all pass away. Be thankful for that in itself – that you have this chance, this opportunity. No matter what your situation is, there is always going to be good and bad; it all depends on your outlook. Just like the missed, last-second field goal, are you looking for the good in the situation? God will only give you what you can handle and no more.

In the world's eye, the kicker was a loser; however, in God's eye, the kicker was a winner. He gave glory to God and thanked him for an incredible opportunity. The world's eyes are much different than God's eyes. When we see life in the way God sees it, we are much happier.

As God spoke to Joshua in Chapter 1, verse 7, "You need only to be strong and courageous and to obey to the letter every law Moses gave you, for if you are careful to obey every one of them, you will be successful in everything you do."

If you see the world as God sees it, in all aspects of life, you will be successful. It may not always seem this way – since the world sees things differently than God does; however, in the end, you will be a success, and the happiness in your life will be so much greater.

How can you be happier with your faith? It's the ability to see through God's eyes that will bring you happiness with your faith.

It's not about the building or about agreeing with everything the church discusses. It's not about having to go to church all the time. It's about the people and the community. If you don't necessarily like or enjoy the church you presently attend, try another one. Church is only one day or one hour a day, if that. The other days and hours are much more important. If you just go to church and don't live the spiritual life outside of church, what good is that? Living the spiritual life, caring for others, loving each other, and looking out for each other is what life is all about.

A professional photographer put it like so: "Actions speak louder than words. Practice what you preach; otherwise, it means nothing. I put my faith in God. Do things in God's name and with a pure heart, and you are doing His will."

An interviewee who was 100-years-old, and one who was sixteen years old, had the same response to the question: "What makes you successful and happy with your spiritual life?" Their answers included the ideas of being active, involved, and making contributions in some way.

What does it mean to be active? It may mean being on parish council. It may mean volunteering to help out with the food pantry. It may mean being a mentor to somebody. It may mean being a big brother or big sister. It may mean all of these things and many others. It's really up to you what you are going to do. It also doesn't necessarily mean doing something within the confines of the church. It's about helping others and treating others as one's self. Not only will it make you happy, but it will make others happy and others will see the good you are doing and try to do the same.

What does it mean to be involved? It really could be all the same as being active; however, it's about being there – wherever that is. It's not just about showing up. It's about actively participating. It may be as simple as being there for your child's tee-ball game or play at school. Your child will obviously enjoy having you there, but you have to be involved. You can't be there and be on your phone doing something else. Even though this isn't something you are doing for the church or with the church, you are contributing to somebody else, and that is part of leading a good and spiritual life.

What does it mean to contribute? It could mean all of the above. It's about helping others. It's about being there when needed. It's about doing something for the community. It's about giving of your time. It's about showing compassion and having gratitude. It could be a simple act of kindness. If it will make somebody else happy, you will be happier for it!

These same traits came up in just about every conversation.

A personal trainer put his own spin on it. "Faith is like exercise; you have to practice it daily and make it part of your lifestyle. It's not just going to church four to five times a year on holidays. Going to church is good, but it's small compared to the other six days of the week."

Speaking about this subject with a successful business owner, he stated he is still searching for what faith means in his own life. He also said that you must sow the field before you harvest it. The Bible says in Galatians 6:7-8 – "For he that soweth to his flesh shall of the flesh reap corruption; but he that soweth to the Spirit shall of the Spirit reap life everlasting."

You will benefit or suffer based on your actions. Do good, and good will come to you; do bad, and bad will come to you.

It's a journey that you are on with your spiritual life. You keep leaning and growing. A veteran who served in Desert Storm stated: "You don't have to preach. It's about private time with daily prayer and dedication. Don't be afraid to show your faith, but you don't have to flaunt it. It's a gift that we have been given."

You must be a light to the world. You must shine and show your best to others. Even when others are not the best, you must still shine. When others are mean, it's really hard not to return that to them. However, it is at this time that you must be as nice as you are rather than being as mean as they are. This will increase your happiness, and most importantly decrease your frustration with your own self. Most of the time, you may get frustrated with yourself by your own doing. You get upset because of how you treat others when you really don't mean to, but you do it because you're taking your frustrations out on others. When this begins to happen, you must stop and cool your thoughts for just a moment before doing something for which you will be sorry.

"Returning violence for violence multiplies violence,

adding a deeper darkness to a night already devoid of stars.

Darkness cannot drive out darkness; only love can do that.

Hate cannot drive out hate; only love can do that."

Martin Luther King

Which is the first of all commandments? Jesus gives his answer: "You shall love the Lord your God with all your heart, with all your soul, with all your mind, and with all your strength." The second is this: "You shall love your neighbor as yourself." The love of God and neighbor are really the same. If you love God, but hate your neighbor, you are not living God's words.

To be truly happy in your faith, you must see others as yourself. Treat others like you want to be treated. It's the Golden Rule. You are no better than anybody else, and nobody else is better than you are. Everyone is equal.

Speaking with Michael, who is nearing retirement, on this subject, he told me this story:

In my first job out of college, working for a radio station and sell-ing advertising, I was selling a promotion to a clothing store in Waterloo, Wisconsin. I was about as raw and green as you can imag-ine. Surprisingly, he said he would buy some advertising. As I was reaching for my pen so he could sign the contract, he noticed I was shaking since I was so nervous. Remember, I was fresh out of col-lege and didn't know much. The owner said, 'Don't be nervous; I'm no better than you.' I couldn't believe it. Not only did he buy some advertising, but he gave me a valuable life lesson all at the same time.

That owner may as well have been reading straight out of the Bible in John 13:16-20. "Amen, amen, I say to you, no slave is greater than his master nor any messenger greater than the one who sent him. If you understand this, blessed are you if you do it." It is essential to have and live an attitude of humility. Even those who know this must still live it, as everyone is equal in the eyes of God.

While discussing this topic with people, the same views were expressed when asked what made them successful and happy with their faith: "It's a work in progress." "It's a life-long journey." "I keep growing & learning." "I'm still searching." "Helping others." A retired HR professional said: "Everyone can be a kinder and gentler version of ourselves." He went on to say, "It's like a workout. Sometimes I really don't want to go to church, but I feel a lot better after I do."

This person hit the nail on the head. How many times do you know you should do something, but you don't? It may be just the easy way out. It may be because you think you don't have the time. However, when you actually do it, you feel so much better. It's the same way with faith. It's the same way with daily life. It seems like there are so many things to do that you don't take the time for the most important things. It's like when you put things off, all of a sudden you have so much to do and don't know where to start. Sometimes life itself gets in the way. There is only so much time in each day. That is why you have to do the important stuff first; otherwise, you might not get to it.

Spirituality and religious involvement link to greater well-being and happiness. Prayer is important. Many people interviewed said it helped relieve stress. A married couple who lost three children during their lives turned to prayer to make it through the tough times. They still had tears in their eyes discussing their losses so many years later. It continues to be hard on them, but they know bad things happen, and with prayer, they are able to get through it.

Each morning when you get up, you may say a little prayer. Each night before you go to sleep, you may thank God for the day you had. When you take a break at work, you may thank your lucky stars that you had the opportunity to work. Be thankful for what you have rather than what you don't have, just like the kicker who missed the field goal.

Fastest Way to Failure and Unhappiness with Your Faith

"When I do good I feel good,

when I do bad I feel bad;

and that's my religion."

Unknown

It's a pretty simple concept. When you do good, you feel good. When you do bad, you feel bad. Doesn't it seem like when you are good, good things happen to you? And, when you do bad, bad things happen to you? When you do bad, you're bound to fail in your faith. It you're not seeing through God's eyes, in terms of what God sees and how God sees, then you're not living your happiest life. What does God see that you don't? He sees everybody as equal. He sees the best in all things. Even when things are not as you want them to be, trust that God is there for you and will help you get through whatever is happening.

Know that bad things are still going to happen. Just like the Bears kicker who wasn't trying to miss the field goal, you're going to make mistakes. Own them, and still thank God for the opportunity you have as you work to be better next time. Simply trying to be better will get you to where you want to go. It will always be a work in progress and a life-long journey. Keep growing and learning.

It's about living and obeying God's commandments. It's about treating others like you want them to treat you. Having compassion for others and helping your family, friends, neighbors, and even complete strangers helps you to live the life that God has called you to live. Your happiness will not be as great as it could be otherwise. Love your neighbor as you love yourself.

Like God says in John, Chapter 15, verses 17-19: "I demand that you love each other, for you get enough hate from the world…!"

Be thankful for what you have right now. Be happy that you get to wake up and start another day. Be happy you get to try to improve upon yesterday. Maybe you made some mistakes; everyone does. But you get to correct those and move forward. If you're not thanking God for your good fortune, then your happiness will not be as great as it could be. Just like everybody else, there will be days when you fail. On these days, still thank God for your good fortune and the opportunities you have.

Ways to Be Happier with Your Faith:

- **Get Involved** – Pray, even if it's just by taking a little time during the day. Volunteer at your church, community organization, or club.

- **Show Gratitude** – Be thankful for what you have. Show and express your appreciation to others. Be a kinder and gentler version of yourself.

- **Find a Mentor** – It could be somebody you know, or a friend of a friend. Ask around. Don't be shy. People are glad to share their experiences and advice.

- **Don't Give Up** – It's a life-long journey. Just because you may disagree with some aspects of life doesn't mean you should throw everything away. Try different churches and communities until you find the right one for you.

- **Reflect** – Use quiet time to think about and study your beliefs. Read the Bible and apply the lessons to your own life.

"The happiness of most people we know is not ruined by great catastrophes or fatal errors, but by the repetition of slowly destructive little things."

Ernest Dimnet,
French priest, lecturer, and author (1866–1954)

How to Be Happier with Your Health and Wellness

Ernest Dimnet's quote sums it up pretty well when it comes to happiness with health and wellness. Most of the time it's the little things, either good or bad, that add up over time and take their toll. Most of the time, it's not something big that helps or hurts; it's all of the little things that come to the forefront. Doing just a little bit better over a long period of time adds up. When you hear somebody say it's the little extra that gets us from ordinary to extraordinary, this is what is being referenced. A little extra can go a long way.

Speaking with a personal trainer, Rob Rufflo, who earned his pro card from the World Natural Bodybuilding Federation, he said to "eat what you want, just not everything all the time. Have balance and take it slow because it takes time." He said to be active every day, even if it's just a little bit. He got to be where he is because his dad was a competitive lifter and marathon runner, so he was around it all the time while growing up, leading him to get involved, too. Even if you didn't grow up with it, you can still take advantage by finding a workout buddy, joining a gym, or finding someone to run with in your spare time.

Doing just a little bit on a consistent basis will add up over time and you will see a big difference in your health and happiness. When you work out, even for a short time, endorphins are released in your body. Endorphins are chemicals that help you feel better and bring about a sense of well-being. They make you feel good and happy. That's why after a good workout, you feel better about yourself. Even if it's just a walk with your dog or a simple walk around the block on your own, do this consistently and you'll feel so much better about yourself.

Just like the personal trainer said to take it slow because it takes time, consider a quote from one of the world's most famous investors, Warren Buffett. He said. "What you do now affects you in ten, twenty, even thirty years." Of course, he was speaking of investing money, but the same can be said about health. What you do today affects you ten, twenty, and even thirty years from now. Just like investing a little bit each day and each year with your money adds up over the long haul, the same is true with your health. Do just a little bit each day, and it adds up over time, for the good. More importantly, it really adds up if you don't do anything, for the worse.

Being in good health is important to being happy. If you look at yourself and don't like what you see, it can be pretty tough to be happy. Just like most things in life, good health is a life-long journey. It takes discipline each day to be happy with your health. Just like all of the other aspects of happiness, it will have ups and downs. Some days will be better than others. The most important thing is to keep going and not give up. Keep trying to improve. Do a little bit each day, and it will make a huge difference down the road.

A lot of people associate health and wellness with working out and being in good physical shape. That is a big part of it, but there is much more to it.

In interviews, when talking about health and wellness, many people talked about how they are happy with how they feel in different terms than working out. Many brought up how they laugh a lot to stay healthier and happier. It makes them feel good to laugh, and many times, it is even at themselves for foolish things they have done. They don't take themselves too seriously. Of course, there's a time and place for being serious, but most of the time, it is important not to take life so seriously. Even just smiling can improve mood and health. It actually spurs a chemical reaction in the brain, releasing hormones like dopamine and serotonin that increase feelings of happiness, and reduce stress. Try it. Smile. It's hard to be in a bad mood when you smile.

Many interviewees stated how they take care of their mental health as a means of achieving happiness with their wellness. One administrator said her "self-care" included just being on her own on a regular basis and doing nothing. She said taking a break was a big part of staying healthy, in addition to getting a solid good night of sleep.

Another interviewee said he schedules a date night with his wife once a week to take a day off from exercise. He also stated that when he needs an emotional break, he will sit and read. He still works out, but he realizes he needs an emotional break every once in a while, too, for his own well-being.

An interesting quote came from a police officer when he was asked about his happiness with his health and wellness. He said, "Growing old is mandatory, growing up is optional, love life!" He meant that even though you might be getting older, it doesn't mean you can't still have fun and enjoy yourself once in a while. He still eats the things he wants to eat, just not all the time. He also mentioned that it's important to respond to what your body tells you. If you don't feel well when you run long distances, try shorter runs and then walking. He also said when he eats in moderation, he feels so much better than after a huge meal.

When an owner of a personal fitness studio was asked how he stays happy with his health and wellness, he said, "Eating and exercise are important, but so is keeping things in perspective when it comes to stress. Stress compared to what? Does it compare to someone looking for food?" He meant to say that you really should not be so stressed about the little things, like when there's no milk for your coffee or when someone cuts you off on the highway. This is especially true when you compare these issues to what others may be going through in their own lives. It's an important component to your happiness with health and wellness. When you stress, you tend to eat worse and work out less. It takes a toll on you, both mentally and physically.

These ideas were brought up time and time again in research for this book. It is about not only your body, but also your mind. Many spoke about how important their mental health is in terms of their happiness with their overall health and well-being. A lot of times, mental health is associated with negative thoughts. However, mental health is all about emotional, psychological, and social well-being. It affects how we think, feel, and act. It helps determine how we handle stress, relate to others, and make choices.

When you feel good about yourself, you tend to make better decisions, handle stress better, and even relate to others better. How do you get to feeling better about yourself in terms of health and wellness? The first thing to realize is you don't have to be a pro athlete to be happy about it. If you want to be a pro athlete, go for it. Realize, though, that less than two percent of college athletes actually make the pros, according to the NCAA. However, don't let this stop you though from making a go of it on a different basis. There are many forms of competition you can compete in without becoming a professional athlete.

You can compete in running, body-building, biking, cross-training, or any of the many activities available. You don't even have to compete against anybody but yourself to be happy about it. Just getting better a little bit day-by-day will improve your overall health and well-being to the point of making yourself feel not only happier, but healthier.

One customer service representative explained it like so: "My dream growing up was to be a wide-receiver in the NFL. I just was never big or strong enough and only played tackle football for two years. But now I get to live my dream of being an athlete every time I go to the gym to work out."

Even though the actual dream this person had was not met, he was still able to live the dream, just in a different way. It's all about perspective.

Another important question is what motivates people to strive for and stay in good health?

When asked about staying in good shape, a former professional football player said, "I work out regularly. The motivation comes from the death of my father when he was 43 and I was 20 years old."

He didn't want to die an early death, but just as important, he didn't want his children to go through what he did. Motivation to stay in good shape and be happy with one's health can come from a lot of different places. Many times, it does come from seeing somebody we know go through a major health scare, or even death.

Another interview with an ex-Olympic athlete brought about this response when he was asked how he still stays happy with his health: "I make working out fun, not hard. I make exercising enjoyable for me." If you enjoy running, run. If you enjoy walking, walk. Whether its golf, cross-country skiing, hiking, biking, yoga, weight-lifting, swimming, or jumping rope, the main thing is to stay active and focus on the positive. There will be some ups and downs along the way. Celebrate the successes you have, and put any negatives in the past.

In terms of eating as it relates to our overall health and happiness, the main theme that was garnered from interviews was this: moderation.

At the time of his interview and 91-years of age, Bill Wambach, who competed many times in the National Senior Games simply said, "I don't overeat." He said he tried to be active every day. He didn't need to do a lot of exercising, but he did do a little bit each day, keeping things in balance and not overdoing it. Having the discipline to stay on course is a vital component of staying happy with your health and wellness.

A doctor of thirty-nine years who has been married for over seventy years discussed this topic said he was definitely successful in his relationship, but he also said he wasn't good at making money since he didn't charge enough in his practice and he paid his associates more, leaving him to take just what he needed. He got a good financial advisor to help him. The key to his happiness was helping others, and in turn, he received all of the help he needed. As far as being happy with his health, he said, "I just take care of myself by doing what I'm supposed to do, and when I'm ill, I listen to what my doctor tells me." While pretty simple advice, it resonates.

Having some balance in terms of happiness with your health was another main theme that was brought up over and over again. It's about creating time for things you have to do and things you want to do.

You want to stay home and binge your favorite TV show, but you know you should really go work out. This is where the balance comes in. Go ahead and binge that TV show and work out a little bit longer tomorrow. Or, have a shorter work out today and still binge that TV show tonight. The bottom line is that you can still do what you want to do while you do what you need to do.

When it comes to health and wellness, it's about knowing your limits and not going to extremes. It's about knowing when it's too much, whether it's about a workout or a diet. One drink every so often may be okay for you, but when you have too many, it may not be so good. When you're just too tired to work out, it may be time for a rest rather than putting your body through another session. You know you should eat more fruits and vegetables, but steak is so good. Have some balance. Enjoy the steak once in a while, but have some fruit and vegetables with every meal.

Fastest Way to Failure and Unhappiness with Your Health and Wellness

"The chief cause of failure and unhappiness is trading what you want most for what you want now."

Zig Ziglar,
Author, salesman & motivational speaker (1926–2012)

When you trade what you want most (being happy and healthy) for what you want now (laziness, TV, or junk food), you end up with just what you don't want – being unhappy and unhealthy. Additionally, when you add this up over time, you end up with more unhappiness, unhealthiness, and most importantly, regret about what you did to yourself. It's so easy to skip that workout. It's so easy to just go to the fast-food restaurant instead of cooking. It's so easy to just do nothing. But it is the fastest way to failure and unhappiness, especially when it comes to health.

Doing a lot of nothing over a long period of time will add up to more than just nothing. It adds up to a life that will be unhealthy and unhappy. As discussed earlier, there is a time to just do nothing – possibly after a hard workout or a long day. You definitely need rest, as this is important to your health. However, when you do nothing good for your health over an extended period of time, it's a good way to experience a lot of negatives with your body. When you don't get a lot of sleep, you end up not performing as well at work, and this leads to less happiness there. You also end up, most likely, eating worse than you would if you had enough rest. It all adds up over time.

After a long, hard day at work, how many times do you just skip the workout and head home? Every so often, this is good to do, as you may need a day off, and most likely a mental break, from the stress at work. But, wouldn't it take a lot of stress away if you worked off that long day at work with a nice workout or a nice walk to get away from it all and smell the fresh air? Even though you don't "feel like" working out, you know you will feel better after you have done so.

Consistency can be good or bad when it comes to your health. If you are consistently putting bad food in your body, it's not going to be good for your health and wellness. Stop causing your own unhappiness with your health by sabotaging yourself. Feel good about yourself by doing a little bit each day. Eat in moderation and stay balanced.

Do what you need to do, so then you can do what you want to do.

Ways to Be Happier with Your Health and Wellness:

- **Eat in Moderation** – Enjoy what you want to eat, but don't stuff yourself. You'll feel better.

- **Laugh and Smile** -- Do not take yourself so seriously all the time. When you feel upset or moody, take a deep breath and smile. It's hard to be upset when you smile.

- **Be Consistent** – Do something on a regular basis. Find something you enjoy and do that. Find a friend who will keep you motivated. Do little things – it takes time.

- **Do Nothing** – Every so often, take a break to just get away. Do something just for you. Get a good night's sleep.

- **Listen to Your Body** – If your body doesn't respond well to a certain workout, try something else. Don't be a stranger to the doctor's office.

The author (right) with Wisconsin Badger Legend, former NFL player, and
College Football Hall of Famer, Pat Richter (left). He was a first-round pick
of the Washington Redskins in the 1963 NFL draft and played eight seasons
in Washington.

Rob Rufflo, ACE certified personal trainer

The author (right) with Bill Wambach (left), 91 at the time, a member of the Wisconsin Senior Olympics Hall of Fame. Not only was he a true track and field superstar – he lived a Hall of Fame life! R.I.P.

"If you look to others for fulfillment, you will never be fulfilled. If your happiness depends on money, you will never be happy with yourself. Be content with what you have; rejoice in the way things are. When you realize there is nothing lacking, the world belongs to you."

Lao Tzu,
ancient Chinese philosopher

Become Happier with Your Money & Finances

You don't have to be a millionaire to be happy with your money. Money can't buy happiness, but $1.56 million can buy Albert Einstein's happiness theory. Two notes written by the famous physicist sold in 2017 for well above their expected value at a Jerusalem auction house. During Einstein's trip to Japan in 1922 to receive the Nobel Prize in Physics, he wrote notes on how to live a fulfilling life. When a messenger came to his room at the Imperial Hotel in Tokyo, he gave him two of the autographed notes because he didn't have any money for a tip. He even said the notes could be worth more than a tip one day.

One note, written in German, translates as: "A calm and modest life brings more happiness than the pursuit of success combined with constant restlessness."

What was Mr. Einstein trying to say? Be happy with what you have and you will have more happiness rather than trying to always get more and more. He did say you can still pursue success, but don't combine it with constant restlessness. Basically, it amounts to being happy and content with what you have while you still go after all you want.

One interviewee had this to say: "You can't be a slave to possessions. Show me your calendar and your checkbook and you show me your priorities. You can't buy things to make you happy. A new car might be new for three months; then what?"

This was a common theme with this topic. Don't get caught up with the Joneses. It's easy to look at others and wish you had what they have. It sometimes seems like the grass is always greener on the other side, but this is not always the case. You may not know the entire situation of the other side. What may look good on the outside may not be so good on the inside. When you concentrate on what others have and what you don't, you miss out on what you actually have.

One young banking professional put it this way when asked about her happiness with money: "I feel like too many people have credit card debt and extra possessions they don't need and can't afford. That's more stress than having what you can afford. We don't live beyond our means, which allows us to be happy."

How do you resist the urge to spend, or over-spend, when it's all around you? Just like the young professional above and many others like her, it's about having what you can afford. Then, you eliminate all of the stress that comes with not being able to afford all you have. Many put it this way: just wait a few days to buy something you want. More often than not, you'll likely realize you don't actually need it. This saves you money, but more importantly, it saves you stress that over-spending brings.

Many had the same attitude, such as the person who said, "My philosophy is that it was too hard to earn the money, so I am more cautious about how it is spent." It's not easy to make money, so when you do make it, make sure you don't waste it. You don't want to waste your time, so why would you want to waste your money? Even people who work in the banking industry, who know about money, still know you have to spend it sometimes. One bank manager stated, "When things change, I have to change my spending habits too, but I also reward myself from time to time." It's okay to spend the money you have on things you want once in a while, as long as you have money for the things you need. Or, as a woman who works in the financial world helping others with their money stated: "There are events I don't expect to happen and things I can't always plan for, so when that happens, I have to cut back on spending or work a little more."

On a consistent basis the same thing was said when asked about happiness with money: Pay attention to savings and be disciplined. Also, finding a way to make it easy on yourself was brought up much of the time. This all ties together. Save on a consistent basis. The way to make it easy is to do it automatically. Set up your savings so when you get paid, a percentage automatically goes to savings.

You don't have to do anything. You don't even see the money; it just gets deposited in your savings account each paycheck. One couple, who never really made a lot of money through the years but has been able to save enough for their golden years, put it this way: "We started our own 'slush fund' so in case there was an emergency, we had money, and if we wanted to treat ourselves to something nice, we had the money, too."

Being somewhat conservative, frugal, saving what you can, adjusting when needed, being disciplined, and simply paying attention were all brought up when discussing people's happiness with their money situations. One gentleman said it even takes a little luck since sometimes there are circumstances out of one's control. He gave the example of an unexpected illness that may wreak havoc on your finances. He continued by saying this is one of the reasons he "gives back" by donating to worthy causes when he can since he considers himself lucky to be in good health as well as good spirits. Now, the question is how some people get lucky and others seem to have no luck at all? Many times, it's about making your own luck, especially when it comes to money. It's about living within your means, saving on a consistent basis, and protecting yourself by saving for the unexpected. We don't want to use insurance – especially life insurance – but it is nice to have when your car gets into an accident or when there is an illness, injury, or permanent disability.

Giving back when you have the opportunity was brought up more than once in reference to happiness. Though, it wasn't always about giving money. Many times, people gave of their time and talents when the opportunity arose.

An interesting message that was brought up many times was how people didn't think they were entitled to what they don't have, or what they had not earned. Hard work was a big part of having what they wanted, much like the gentleman who said he worked too hard for his money to waste it. By not wasting money, you can still enjoy the things you want. By taking care of your needs first, you can then take care of your wants. You may not get everything you want all at once, but you'll eventually get there.

One night, while flipping channels, I came across an interview with a legendary rock n' roll artist, Brian Johnson, who told the story of how he was done with the band he was playing with and how he was looking for work. He saw an ad for work replacing windshields. The ad said to meet the salesman in a park and just knock on the window to talk. He thought this was about as low as it could get, so he did not go. He was going to go back to his old job, but he thought he would be made fun of since he had been living the life of a rock n' roll singer. Then, one day, out of the blue, he received a call for a tryout with a different band. The band turned out to be ACDC, and the rest is history. It was his big break. He loved singing and touring. The one thing he did not enjoy was the fame. He discussed how he used to go to a local pub and have a drink. Then, when success came, he went there and was really shocked. The regulars he used to drink with had changed, even though he had not. They kind of turned their noses up at him. They said things like, "How come you're coming in here flaunting all your money?" He wasn't doing any such thing. He was doing what he had always done, just having a drink. The difference was that his old "buddies" were jealous of his success.

There are many people who just don't want to see others succeed, especially if the achievement is more success than they themselves have. It's just the opposite of trying to keep up with the Joneses – some people can't handle others having more than they have. It's too bad, but this is too often the case. If you can't celebrate others' successes and be truly happy for them, then you lose out on a lot of your own happiness. You can still strive to be better, but it doesn't mean you can't appreciate what you already have and what others have.

One song from ACDC is titled "Money Talks." It sounds like a salute to money, but it's just the opposite; it's a jab at those who flaunt their wealth and how money divides us. The band was very rich, but they didn't flaunt their wealth; they stayed grounded. Looking at the other side – if you don't have a lot of money, don't turn your nose up at those who do. Enjoy what you have and be grateful for your own gifts.

When we say someone is "wealthy," what are we really saying? Wealth implies abundance. But there are different kinds of wealth. In the Bible story of the Rich Young Man who wanted to follow Jesus, he had an abundance of material goods. What he didn't have, according to Father Grant Thies from the Diocese of Madison Wisconsin, was a deep sense of meaning, purpose, and interior peace for which he longed. Father Thies says, "To be truly fulfilled as human beings, we must fill our souls with virtue, with an abundance of repeated choices that reflect moral integrity, not moral decadence." He went on to say, "We tend to think that we could solve all our problems if we just had enough money. Money cannot solve all our problems. The classic movie 'It's a Wonderful Life' reminds us of this. The richest man in town, Mr. Potter, is also the most miserable – by far. Whereas the man who is always just barely getting by, George Bailey, is Bedford Falls' most valued and beloved citizen. True wealth goes beyond money."

This was very revealing. When discussing this topic with a number of individuals and couples, not one person said they were happy with their financial situation because they made a lot of money. There was one gentleman in particular who even said he has had many opportunities to make more money, but that was not his goal. It wasn't his "why." Others have told him to do this or that to make more money. He always says no. His "why" is his family. He could make more money and spend less time with his family, but he wants to spend more time with his wife and kids.

You can even take this a step further. Spending your money and time on others may even make you happier. Laurie Santos, psychology professor at Yale University, says, "There's lots of research showing that spending our time and money on other people can often make us happier than spending that same time or money on ourselves." She is also the teacher of the school's most popular course: "Psychology and the Good Life."

While interviewing one gentleman on this subject, he said one day his son asked him: "How do you know if you are rich?" His answer was quite compelling and he says he continues to have the same discussion with him to this day. He said, "You won't know during your life if you are rich. You will only find out after you pass away. You'll find out then if you have touched people and they celebrate your time together while at your funeral. So, son, when I pass away, look up and let me know if I was rich." He went on to say that if you live the right way, you have a good chance to be rich.

Living the right way means having gratitude toward others – showing appreciation for others and returning their kindness. Be thankful for the friends and family you have. Listen to others and have a genuine interest in what they have to say. Be willing to compromise with others to see their point of view. There is more to being happy with your money and finances than just the money you make. There are different kinds of wealth. More money can't buy more happiness. Yes, you need some money to make ends meet, but real wealth goes far beyond the money you have.

Fastest Way to Failure and Unhappiness with Your Money and Finances

"It is not the man who has too little,

but the man who craves more, that is poor."

Seneca the Younger,
Roman statesman (circa 5 B.C. – A.D. 65)

To be truly happy with your money and finances, you must be grateful for what you already have and not look to what others have that you don't. You must not try to keep up with the Joneses, as they say. If you are not grateful for what you already have, you will never be happy with what you do have. If you are constantly comparing yourself to others, you are not going to be happy. You may not even know what you have since you will be so obsessed with what others possess.

Speaking with a financial specialist in Montana, she said; "I've been asked why I am such a positive person, considering the adversity I've experienced. For me, it's simply appreciating what I have instead of what I don't have in my life. For example, last week was full of highs and lows. Instead of focusing on the lows or letting them control me, I chose to embrace the highs." If you focus on the negatives, on what you don't have, you lose out on what you actually do have. Your happiness will not be as great as it could be. Instead of focusing on what others have, make it a priority to focus on what you already have as you try to go after all you want. It's okay to strive for more, just don't forget what you already enjoy.

Many times, also, we are in a hurry to get what we want. We want a bigger house, a newer car, and everything all at once. However, when we are in a hurry, many times that is when we make mistakes, especially when it comes to our money and finances. "Hurry. Time is running out" is a slogan you hear and see all the time with sales. It's a way to create a sense of urgency to tempt people before they have a chance to make an informed decision.

How many times are you in such a rush that you forget something? It may be in the morning as you get ready for work. Or, it could be when you are running many errands after work so you can get home faster. The more in a rush you are, the better your chances are to make a mistake. If you forget something at the grocery store, it really isn't that big of a deal. However, if you are in a rush to make a financial decision, it could be far worse. Take a break from it and go back to it in a few days. Give it time and see if you really need to buy that item, invest that stock, etc. You may be surprised at the result.

Ways to Be Happier with Your Money & Finances:

- **Have Gratitude** – Be grateful for what you already have and strive to go after all you want. Concentrate on what you do have rather than what you don't have.

- **Be Consistent with Savings** – Save what you can on a regular basis even if it's just for a rainy day. Take advantage of any employers' savings plan, especially if they offer matching funds

- **Give Back** – When you have the opportunity to donate money to a cause you believe in, take advantage of it. Also, if money is tight, remember that you can donate your time and talents.

- **There's More to Wealth Than Money** – Money can't solve all of your problems. Being rich with other gifts such as family and friends is more rewarding than the items money can buy.

- **Get Help from a Professional** – Schedule an appointment with a trusted financial advisor. Ask a friend or neighbor for a referral. If you can't figure something out on your own, stop spinning your wheels and ask for help.

"Gratefulness is the key to a happy life we hold in our hands, because if we are not grateful, then no matter how much we have we will not be happy – because we will always want to have something else or something more."

David Steindl-Rast,
author and lecturer

52 Week Challenge to Reach the "Happy Zone"

Gratitude is defined in the dictionary as the quality of being thankful; readiness to show appreciation for and to return kindness. It is the state of being grateful. Even if you are not necessarily returning kindness, you can give kindness just as a way to make others and yourself happy. This chapter gives you some ideas of what you can do to hand out kindness – fifty-two ways, to be exact. Go through the list and pick out one to complete each week to make somebody's day a bit brighter. By doing this, you'll find yourself in a happier place.

1. **Pay it forward** –You could pay for lunch for the next person in line. You can donate your money or talents to a cause about which you feel strongly.

2. **Choose to be happy** – No matter the situation, this is a good rule of thumb. It may not be the best of situations, but you can find a way to be happy no matter what is happening. This week, even if someone else is a grouch, choose to be happy.

3. **Focus** – What you focus on the longest becomes the strongest. Focus on the positives, not what you might have to do later.

4. **Take your time** – Make space to just breathe and be still. Slow down as you rush through the day. Walk a little slower and take it all in.

5. **Leave a positive note for someone** – It may be your husband, wife, child, or co-worker. Let them know, even with a small Post-it note, how you feel about them and what they mean to you.

6. **See another perspective** – Even if you don't agree with it, you can at least think about how the other side feels and understand where they are coming from in terms of a topic that has been bothering you.

7. **Have a child-like wonder** – Be like a kid: appreciate the little wonders of life. Be awed by snowflakes and flowers, and believe in magic.

8. **Be enthusiastic** – Have enjoyment and show interest in what you are doing.

9. **Say thank you and you're welcome** – When someone does something for you – no matter how big or small – say thank you; it will automatically make you feel better. The same goes for "you're welcome" when someone says "thank you" to you.

10. **Celebrate** – Do something to celebrate an accomplishment this week or just because – there is no need for it to be anything big. Go out and celebrate just for the fun of it.

11. **Give clothes away** – You know you have some clothes you have not worn in years. Get them out and give them away. Someone needs them and will use them.

12. **Get back to basics** – Eat well, exercise, and go to bed a bit earlier. You'll feel more refreshed and happier.

13. **Dress up** – Decide to make yourself look a little bit better than usual, just for the heck of it.

14. **Write it down** – At the end of each day, write down three things that were good about that day. They don't have to be mind-blowing.

15. **Don't take it personally** – When it seems someone is upset with you, remember it's not you. It's their situation, not yours. Don't treat them as bad as they are, treat them as good as you are.

16. **Stay in touch** – Write a letter, or better yet, give a phone call to someone you haven't seen or spoken to in a while.

17. **Don't worry** – Put your worries aside, especially about issues you cannot control.

18. **Be yourself** – Don't compare yourself to others. Be who you are. Express yourself and how unique you are.

19. **Watch yourself** – This includes your language, your thoughts, and your choices. Be positive in all you do.

20. **Do nothing** – At least for the weekend, free up your calendar and make no plans. Be carefree, and go with the flow.

21. **Share your talents** – Whether it's at work or in your free time, share your talents with someone by helping with something they need.

22. **Meditate** – At the end of each day, take time for yourself to think deeply and focus in silence for at least a few minutes.

23. **Be appreciative** – In all you do, appreciate what you have, and don't take people for granted.

24. **Get involved** – No grand act is needed; whatever you are doing, be there in totality. It may be something you've wanted to do, so get involved in it. Or it may be something you have been missing, like simply helping your husband, wife, or child with a chore.

25. **Be thankful for food** – Don't take it for granted. And, slow down when you eat. How many times have you rushed though lunch or dinner? Enjoy it, and be thankful for those who made it possible.

26. **Plan your next vacation/stay-cation** – Plan your next get-away, even if it's just staying at home for a few days. What do you want to do? Where do you want to go?

27. **Stay calm in the storm** – When things don't go your way, take a deep breath and stay calm. Most likely it won't matter in a year or two, so don't get so uptight over it.

28. **Give someone a compliment** – It may be your wife or husband or a co-worker, but for no reason but to be nice, give that person a compliment. Do this once a day. It may even be a complete stranger, but find a way to say something nice.

29. **Get outside** – Take a walk, look at the flowers, go to the park, take it all in! Give your mind and body a natural boost.

30. **Work on it** – Is there something you have been regretting? Think about it this week and work on changing it. It doesn't have to be life-changing. Maybe you need to cut back on snacks. Or, it might be that you need to forgive yourself for something.

31. **Smile more!** – Even when things are not going your way, flash your smile! You'll be amazed at how much better you feel and how you will make others feel.

32. **No complaining** – This one will take some effort. Make it like the five-second rule when you drop food. If you find yourself complaining, STOP.

33. **Take responsibility** – Do this for your own life, and don't blame others for your mistakes. You're responsible for your own actions, your own accomplishments, and your own happiness.

34. **Be empathetic** – Understand and actually share someone else's feelings. When someone you know, at home or at work, is having a tough day, be there for them.

35. **Set a goal** – Big or small, it doesn't matter. What is something that you want to make happen, whether it is in your career, relationships, health, or another area? This week is when you start toward that goal.

36. **Choose a different route** – Take another route to work for at least one day and see what you notice on the way. Change up your dinner routine just a bit, do something different for lunch, or simply get ready for work the night before so you won't need to rush in the morning.

37. **Use the good china/plates** – One day, get out the good plates, just because. And, if you don't have "good" plates, make an extra special meal.

38. **Help a friend or neighbor** – If you know someone who needs assistance with something, show up and help. If you don't know someone in need, help out a co-worker with a project, mow a neighbor's lawn, take out the garbage, or shovel someone's driveway after a snowfall. Just help out to help; don't wait to be asked.

39. **Keep work at work** – When you come home from work this week, forget about work. Be present with yourself and your family.

40. **Forgive/Let it go** – Don't let it linger any longer. Forgive the person you've not forgiven. Let the past be the past; live in the now.

41. **Concentrate** – Do one thing at a time; concentrate on this, and once done, move on to the next task. Whatever you are doing, do that and nothing else as a means of taking it all in.

42. **Arrange a get-together** – Do this with a friend or with your family. Even if it's just a walk, or you can call or text and make plans to get together for dinner.

43. **Make a list** – Write down your goals for yourself, your career, your family, and anything else that you want to do. This doesn't have to

be earth-shattering. It can be as simple as wanting to be easier on yourself. It's your list, so make it what you want.

44. **Change your language** – Instead of saying "I have to…" say "I get to…" I have to go to work, I have to go grocery shopping, I have to work out – they all sound negative. Instead, say, "I get to go to work (to earn money), I get to go to the grocery store (to have food to eat), and I get to go work out (to stay healthy). Change your mindset to the positive just by changing your words.

45. **Volunteer** – Give of your time at a food pantry. Go to a senior center and offer your time and talents. Pick a cause you care about and make it worthwhile for yourself and others.

46. **Say "I Love You"** – Say this to your significant other, children, parents, or a friend in a way you normally do not. Don't forgo the normal hug and kiss before you go off to work, but add a little extra.

47. **Declutter** – This doesn't seem too glamorous, but it takes only about twenty to thirty minutes to clean up one area. You'll feel so much better about it once you're done. It's not as big a project as it seems. It could be your closet or a junk drawer.

48. **Plan the next day** – Again, this is not such a big deal, but it makes the next morning so much easier. What are you going to wear? Do you need to make a lunch? What do you need to do? What do you want to do tomorrow?

49. **Think of happy memories** – Look back at photos, videos, or yearbooks of past events that brought you happiness. It'll bring back those joyful moments you experienced.

50. **Go after life!** – Seek enjoyment in everything you do. Be fascinated with all things. Take it to a different level than you have in the past! Enjoy the sunrise and sunset. Enjoy the smell in your kitchen when you cook. Enjoy the drive home. Enjoy petting your dog.

51. **Give yourself a pat on the back** – Notice the things that go well, and give yourself well-deserved acknowledgment.

52. **It's a Miracle** – Take to heart this quote from Albert Einstein: "There are two ways to live: You can live as if nothing is a miracle, or you can live as if everything is a miracle."

"The happiest moments in life come from making someone else happy."

John Wooden,
legendary basketball coach

The Common Thread

John Wooden, the legendary UCLA basketball coach, could not have said it better. When we are at our happiest, we are making others happy. When we are at our happiest, we are sharing what we have with others. When we are at our happiest, we are not thinking of just ourselves. This was the "common thread" in all of the conversations and interviews. "What makes you happy?" was the question, and not one time was the answer money. Not one time was the answer success in work. Not one time was it anything other than family and friends.

The resounding, number one answer to the question of "What makes you happy?" was relationships.

It didn't matter if we were discussing a person's career. One answer was, "Coaching a teammate to see their greatness and them having success."

Or, if we were discussing health, one answer was, "Taking a walk with the family and staying healthy for them." Even regarding spiritual life, answers included: "Being a part of a community," and "Helping others through tough times."

It was even there when discussing money. "What's your why? Mine is my family. It's why I work and strive to be my best."

Having relationships, whether at work, at home, or in a place of worship, was what made people happiest. Seeing their kids having success and being happy, along with simply spending time with family and friends, was by far the number one answer to what makes people happy. It was never some grand answer or complicated scheme. It was by far all of the simple things in life. The little things that we take for granted are what made people the happiest. Sharing experiences with loved ones was one of the most common responses.

One couple learned early on not to take life for granted as she was diagnosed with breast cancer in her thirties and was able to beat it. They now live life and each day in the moment. They are present in whatever they are doing and wherever they are. Since then, they take it all in and say, "You can't be happy unless you are in the moment."

Even things as little as what this gentleman said: "Little children looking up and asking their Mom a question … "Mama? And their Mom's looking back down at them with a loving look that only a Mom can give her child and she replies, 'Yes, baby?' This happened to me this weekend," he continued, "while I was standing in line at the library."

It was amazing that almost all of the responses to "What makes you happy?" had very little to do with the individual. One person went so far as to say, "When I isolate myself, I am unhappy." He then said, "I don't want others to be unhappy." He also said to respect each other and others' opinions, even if you don't agree. His number one source of happiness was his kids and seeing them in a happy state. He summed it up this way: "It's important to be involved, get in the game – the game of life!"

Being involved was a key factor, as it's really no different than happiness in relationships. You have to be involved to be in a relationship. You have to listen to people and be interested in what they have to say. Just like the gentleman whose wife had breast cancer said, "You can't be happy unless you are in the moment." Whatever you are doing, you have to be there, and be involved.

One interviewee who works as a carpenter said that family is the number one source of happiness. "With them, I can get through anything. When I come home from a rough day at work, I get to see my family and be with them."

An AP Literature teacher in Houston, Texas said, "This is our one and only shot at life, and we need to go all in."

You can't just do it half-way. You have to do it all the way. Whether it is in your relationships, with your money, in your career, with your health, or with your faith, you must be involved in what you are doing and live in the moment to be happy. It really is our one shot at a happy life. So, why not go all in? You can't take any breath for granted. You never know when you will take your last gasp of air. Use the good china today. Don't wait to go on that trip. Give a big bear hug to your wife or husband and your children. Remember, tomorrow is promised to nobody. But if you do the right things today, you set the stage for a happier tomorrow.

To be involved, you might choose to take a genuine interest in other people. One woman, who received her Master's Degree in French and was married in France, said her book club that has been together for 25 years is a great source of her happiness. They love getting together and not only finding out what everyone thinks about what they read, but finding out how everybody is doing in their lives. She also stated that giving help to others was part of what makes her happy.

Many people mentioned that one source of their happiness was volunteering for a cause near and dear to them. Others simply volunteered with friends and it made them more appreciative of what they already had. They enjoyed being with other volunteers while they assisted in the cause. This really hits the nail on the head. Being with others and enjoying what you have with others is the path to the "happy zone."

When we make others happy is when we are at our happiest. It's not just about you. It's about the other people in your life. It's about appreciating what you have and enjoying what you have with others. It could be with your family or friends or even people you don't know. This is not to say you can't strive for more in your life, but simply be happy where you are as you strive to be better.

One "common thread" was being with other people and appreciating them. It was helping others have success while also appreciating what you personally have. It was being involved in your own life as well as those of others. It had very little to do with individuals and was more about other people. It had more to do with family, friends, and even strangers, rather than ourselves. It was about not taking anything for granted.

It's also trying to be better in all aspect of life. Sharing what you have with others will allow you to live each day in the moment. You will be more present and able to take it all in. You will have hope and want others to be happy, not allowing outside factors determine your happiness. Happiness is truly an "inside" job. It comes from within.

It also has a lot to do with gratitude. Showing appreciation to others and even going so far as having appreciation for what you already have is important. Appreciating our own gifts instead of thinking the grass is greener on the other side is important. It is also about seeing the other side, even if you don't agree with it. Listening is part of the equation all the way around. Not just to the other side, but to people with whom you are closest. Listening means you care about those people.

The "common thread" of happiness can be summed up like this: Being around and involved with your friends and family while appreciating the gifts you have and trying to be a better version of yourself in all aspects of life. If you can weave these ideas into your life on a consistent basis, you have a better chance of reaching the "happy zone."

Fastest Way to Failure and Unhappiness

"Happiness is not the absence of problems,
but the ability to deal with them."

Charles Louis de Montesquieu,
French philosopher (1689–1755)

The French philosopher was right on with his assessment of happiness. It's not always going to be easy. It's not always going to be sunshine and roses. There will be some tough times. However, the goal is to be happier more often and more consistently than you are now. The fastest way to fail is to be angry and upset.

Here is an analogy in the form of a question to help make sense of this: You have $86,400 in your bank account and somebody takes $10 from you. Would you be upset and throw the rest of the money away in hopes of getting back at the person who took the $10 from you? Or, would you move on and live? The best answer is to simply move on. Think about how you have 86,400 seconds in every day, and don't let somebody's negative 10 seconds ruin the rest of the 86,390 other seconds in your day.

Part of being happy is not being angry. The less angry you are, the happier and better off you'll be. Many times during the day, you might focus on the bad stuff that happens and think it outweighs the good. However, in reality, the bad is just a fraction of your time and you are choosing to focus on that instead of all of the good in your life.

One woman, when asked what makes her happy, said, "Not reacting to negative stuff, and having hope in all things, gives me peace and happiness." She went on to say that when something negative does happen, she takes a step back at first rather than reacting right away. This makes her happy since she doesn't get down when negative things do happen. And, negative things *will* happen. It's just the way life goes. You can choose to react in a negative way or you can take a deep breath and stop the negative response.

When somebody is negative toward you, it can be really hard not to be negative back. However, if you respond to negativity on a regular basis, you are going to end up being a "negative nelly" yourself. Nobody is going to want to be around you, and you will be on your way to being really unhappy more times than not. It's the fastest way to failure as far as your happiness is concerned. So, instead of responding like a negative person, respond in a nice way. Instead of acting as badly as they did, respond positively.

Just because you might be a "negative nelly" at certain times doesn't mean you can't change. It's not easy, but it can be done, if you have a desire. Who doesn't want to be happy? One gentleman said he was in this exact position a few years ago. He was not a very positive person and, because of this, he was not very happy. While reading a book one day, he came across a quote that stuck with him: "What the mind can believe and conceive, the mind can achieve with a positive mental attitude." From that point forward, he made each day great no matter what happened during the day. He simply changed his attitude, and it changed his entire life.

How can you keep a positive mental attitude? No matter the circumstances, you make the best of it. You don't let outside factors affect your happiness. You keep a positive attitude even if it's raining outside, because inside, it's always 75 and sunny.

Having a positive mental attitude is really best described as being in "the happy zone." It's where you find happiness in the simplest things, like spending time with family and friends, watching and helping others succeed, sharing your gifts with others, enjoying each day and each breath you have, not worrying about what you don't have, and appreciating what you already have while actively pursuing those things you want. You always want to try, each and every day, to be a better version of yourself.

So, in the next day, month, or year, give it a try. Approach each day with a positive mental attitude. Don't let the negatives bring you down. Don't treat them as bad as they are; treat them as good as you are. You'll see the change, almost immediately, for the better. You'll be able to better handle the negative stuff and not let it spill into all of the positive aspects of life.

*"Be happy with what you have.
Be excited about what you want."*

**Alan Cohen,
Award-winning author**

Ten Things to Do to Enter "The Happy Zone"

Choose your attitude. **Choose** to be positive more times than not. Don't let negative people bring you down. Don't let outside factors determine your happiness.

Live YOUR life. Don't let others judge what should bring you happiness. Happiness must come from inside you. Don't copy somebody else; you may not know that person's entire story. Don't live somebody else's life. Live your life!

Smile. Give it a try. Right now. Smile. It's hard to be in a bad mood when you put your smile on. Do it more often and you'll notice a difference in your level of happiness.

Practice gratitude. It's all about being thankful for what you have. Show appreciation for your own gifts and for those of others. Return others' kindnesses by handing out your own kindness. Be grateful for what you have.

Enjoy the NOW. Be involved in the here and now. Whatever you are doing, do it without worrying about what you might have to do in the future. Be present for yourself and others.

Be prepared. Be ready to deal with whatever comes your way. Get enough sleep so you are ready for the day. Make it easier on yourself so you don't get frustrated. Give yourself time to do what is needed without rushing.

Get up, dress up, and show up. Be enthusiastic for the day. Have passion for what you are doing. Put on your "happy socks."

<u>Slow down.</u> Enjoy all of the little things you might be missing out on. Stop to smell the roses. Enjoy each day. Celebrate just to celebrate.

<u>Forgive.</u> Let it go. Focus on the good. Search for the good. Don't judge. Be slow to anger.

<u>Listen.</u> Do this with both yourself and your body. If it doesn't feel right, then stop doing it. Listen to others and be there for them.

"Happiness is not a station you arrive at,
but a manner of traveling."

Margaret Lee Runbeck,
American author (1905–1956)

Simplicity is the Ultimate Sophistication

When you are a student, sometimes you have a hard time understanding something until somebody shows you how to make the difficult simple. You tend to think that person is really special and a lot smarter than you. That may not be the case. That person most likely just looked at the situation in a different way.

When you can make the difficult easy, it's the ultimate form of sophistication. It's really just a matter of how you look at things. It's similar to when you were in school. If you were like me, you studied so you would do well on the test. You didn't necessarily study to learn. You still had to learn so you would do well on the test, but you didn't necessarily study to learn for the future. You didn't think that you would need the knowledge down the line.

It's the same way with being happy. It's how you look at it, not how somebody else sees it. Just like Margaret Lee Runbeck said, it's "not a station you arrive at, but a manner of traveling." How are you going to travel? Make it simple, and therefore life will be simple. Make it what you want to make it, and don't worry about what others think.

You may look at the rain as a bummer since you were hoping to enjoy the outdoors. However, the farmer is looking at the rain and rejoicing in it since it will help his crops. It's just a different way of looking at the situation.

You may see the missed field goal from your team as a loss, but the coach may look at it as a learning tool for his team to not let the game come down to a last-second field goal. There's a lot more to a game than just the last second. You and the coach are both looking at the same loss, but you're looking at it differently.

You may think driving long-distance for vacation or the holidays is a drag. However, your kids love to look at all of the new scenery and think it's a blast.

You may think mowing the lawn is such a chore, but when you see your neighbor mowing his lawn, it looks like he is actually enjoying it. Your neighbor may be enjoying the outdoors and trying to zone out for a while as he mows.

You may see the snow fall as such an inconvenience, but others just take it a bit slower and see the beauty in it.

Just like earlier when the gentleman was a "negative nelly" until he incorporated the positive mental attitude in his life, we can all look at things more positively and make things simpler for ourselves.

Making things simple will make you feel like a superstar. How do we make it simple to be happy in all areas of life? Here's what we can do:

When it comes to money, make it easy to save. Do it automatically. If you don't see it, you don't spend it. If your employer has a 401k or retirement match, take advantage of it; it's like free money, and you'll be able to watch it grow.

How about your career? Do what you love and you'll never "work" again. Many feel this is easier said than done, but look at it like this – if you're traveling to a certain destination, no matter how long it takes, you can still enjoy the journey. The same is true of your career; you may think of it as a means to an end – your retirement – but you can still enjoy the journey to get there.

You can make your relationships easier, too. Don't dwell on the negatives – enjoy all of the good things that come with your relationships. Enjoy being together, and don't worry about what might happen in the future. Be present. No more nit-picking. Work together and be grateful for each other.

With faith, there's a simple way as well. It's a lifelong journey. Enjoy each day with hope for a better tomorrow. Look at things as God looks at them. See everybody as God sees them. Everybody is equal.

How can you make your health a bit simpler? Get good advice from your doctor, listen to it, and then incorporate it in your daily life. It's not rocket science. It's as simple as listening, learning, and then using that knowledge to live a healthier life.

Remember, there's more than one way to look at every situation. And, there's always more than one solution to a problem. There's more than one road to travel to your destination. It's like the baseball coach who sees his pitcher struggling to get outs early in the game. Most of the time, the coach goes out to offer advice, which mainly amounts to throwing strikes. The pitcher knows this, of course, but instead of stating it this way, one time a coach saw his pitcher struggling, and he went to the mound to give him a hug. This true story happened at a high school baseball game. The coach thought the pitcher could use a hug. And, you know what? He was right. The pitcher settled down, got into a groove, and he played the game much better afterward.

You see, the coach made it easy on his pitcher. He didn't offer up the same advice he may have suggested in the past. The pitcher knew what needed to be done, but he just needed some encouragement. He needed somebody who cared about him and the situation. The coach cared about what was happening to the pitcher and did something about it with that hug. There's no one right way to deal with a situation. It should never just be a cookie-cutter reaction.

Happiness is not some place you go. It is how you travel day to day that leads to happiness. Just as the coach led his player to a more comfortable position on the mound with his hug, you too can lead yourself to a happier place by how you look at things.

When you listen to a song or your favorite artist, do you ever wonder how in the world they can make it sound and look so simple? They make it easy on themselves, too. They break it down into easy steps. When you think about it, it really isn't all that complicated. For example, western music is made up of just twelve tones. They are sometimes called the chromatic scale. This has twelve pitches, each a semitone or half-step above or below adjacent pitches. When you listen to a song, though, it sounds like a lot more than that. Keep it simple and it's a lot easier to understand.

One interviewee put this take on it: "Too often in society we put the 'cart' before the 'horse.' We need to slow down to fully know what is in front of us. Let's all work together to make sure the 'cart' and the 'horse' are in the proper order." He was giving real, simple advice. Before you pray, believe. Before you spend, earn. Before you speak, listen. Before you quit, try. Before you die, live.

Simple words and simple advice. It really is sophisticated.

"The happiness of your life depends on the quality of your thoughts."

Marcus Aurelius the Philosopher

Your "Happy Zone"

Just as the quote above says, "your thoughts" make you the happiest; you get to determine your "Happy Zone." What you think of the most you become, no matter if it's positive or negative, good or bad, healthy or unhealthy. You, and only you, should decide what your "Happy Zone" looks like.

One woman had a great story to tell when it came to what makes her happy. She had just listened to a TED talk titled, "Where Joy Hides and How to Find It." It was about "things" that bring joy and happiness. She said it really made her think about her home. She shared:

Our kitchen has been bright yellow for many years, and covering our kitchen walls were framed, colorful, love-filled artwork that my kids created when they were young. I hung them originally because I loved them; they were colorful and creative, and I was so proud of my kids for making them. I think I also kept them up because they truly brought me joy and happiness. Recently, we decided that it was time to paint the kitchen. There are divots in the walls where the chairs were consistently leaned back on and bumped against, or actual chunks of plaster missing on the corners where the vacuum cleaner bumped as I put it away in the closet. I decided it was time to have a 'grown up' kitchen and take down the kids' artwork. My family voted a strong 'no more yellow.' So, this weekend, we painted over the yellow with a very boring and plain 'cream.' I am not liking it. It is so plain and it is not making me happy. I have spent the evening searching design sites for color combinations and decorating tips, and none of them jump out at me. Then, I watched this video on design that was shared by a colleague of mine; it is about things that bring us joy and happiness just by looking at them, and I suddenly understood. My kitchen might not have been all that fashionable, or grown-up looking, but it brought me joy. My kids' paintings brought me so much joy, and let's not even talk about the eighteen years of names, dates, and heights for three kids and two dogs that are written right on the wall down the hall that I am going to have to paint over – or maybe not. So, I think it's back to the paint store for me to find some new colored paint. I promised the kids nothing yellow, but there are so many other colors.

What "things" make you happy and bring you joy? Does it matter if it's considered "grown-up" or not? Is it only supposed to bring you joy if "others" approve of it?

Is it okay if it's different than the norm? Would life be boring if everybody was the same and did all of the same things? Just because everybody else is doing it, does it mean you have to? Sometimes the road less traveled is better.

You must not let others determine your "Happy Zone". It must be yours. You determine your own happiness. You determine what gets you there. You determine what "things" make you happy. If others don't like it, so be it. Remember, you can agree to disagree. You can still see the other side, but just don't compare yourself to others and don't think you are any better than anybody else. You can still strive to better yourself as you appreciate what you already have.

When the woman was trying to make her kitchen "grown-up," what did she mean? According to the dictionary, grown-up is thought to mean that something is adult, mature, of age, having reached one's majority, full-grown, or fully developed. It almost sounds like "reaching one's majority" is the end of one's life. Or, at least on the way to it. The fact is that grown-ups could be eighteen years of age, and there's a lot of life left as well as a lot of "growing up" to do at that age. No matter the age, you can still learn, progress, get better, and be happy.

Part of the definition of "grown-up" includes "adult." What does that mean? Adult, according to the dictionary, is a person who is fully grown or developed; it is someone who is mature and can still develop mentally and emotionally. If you are forty years old, or "middle-aged," as some would say, you are not necessarily done developing. You may have stopped growing physically, but you are still capable of learning and gaining intelligence.

Nowhere in any of those definitions does it say anything about how you are to act, yet when you are "grown-up," you are expected to act a certain way. This doesn't have to mean being upset all the time or being unhappy, and it doesn't mean not being able to do what you want. Thinking back on the example of the woman and her kitchen, color the kitchen the way you want. Put up the photos. Decorate however you want, not the way you think is expected of you.

It's generally not a good idea to assume things. Just because it's assumed, doesn't mean that it is correct. Many times, if you assume something, you eventually find out you're wrong or somehow incorrect.

Assuming the grass is greener on the other side is one such assumption, but many times when you get to the other side, you find out it's just not true

Do you ever notice how people in your neighborhood put up their Christmas lights way too early? Why do you think it's too early? Why is it too early to celebrate? Why is it too early to feel good? Why is it too early to be festive? If people acted all year like they do at Christmas time, the world would be a much better place. Remember, you don't want others to tell you what makes you happy, so we must not judge others in this way either. If someone wants to put up their Christmas lights early, then let them. Now, I know we're all human and every so often we might catch ourselves judging others, but when this happens, try to take a deep breath and put on a smile. Realize that we're all human, and we're all trying to make the best of our lives.

Another example might be when you see somebody taking a selfie. There was actually a 2016 study which found that selfies increase confidence and make people happier. While some people cringe at the idea of someone taking a selfie, researchers at the Donald Bren School of Information and Computer Sciences asked students from the University of California, Irvine to participate in a study about it. The students were divided into three groups, and each was asked to take a unique series of photos: daily selfies while smiling, photos of items that made them happy, or photos of items they thought would make others happy, which they would share with that person.

The results showed everyone's increased positive moods. The selfie group said they felt more confident and comfortable. The students taking photos of items that made them happy reported feeling more reflective and appreciative, while those taking photos that made others happy said it helped them feel more connected to those people.

"Our research showed that practicing exercises that can promote happiness via smartphone picture taking and sharing can lead to increased positive feelings for those who engage in it," said lead author Yu Chen, a postdoctoral scholar in University of California, Irvine's Department of Informatics.

Give it a try sometime and you can find out for yourself that it not only makes you happier, but it makes other people happy as well. Wouldn't you feel special if somebody wanted to take a photo with you? That's how others feel when you ask to take a photo with them. I've put this to the test many times. I myself have taken probably two-hundred plus selfies. The funny thing is that nobody has ever said no to me. They are always appreciative that I ask them for a selfie. Whether everyday people or celebrities, they can't say no. Even when I take a walk in the neighborhood, I'll see some friends and just grab my phone to take a selfie with them. It makes me happy, and it makes them happy, so why not go ahead and do it?

With country music artist Toby Keith (right). Do you notice the "photo bombers" in the background?

Just walking on the street in San Francisco near Fisherman's Warf and across the street I saw this clown (right). You think he was happy to take a selfie with me? What a clown!

On vacation a few years ago in downtown Louisville, I saw a boxing ring in the middle of the street, and who was there? It's former Heavyweight Champion, Evander Holyfield (left)

Every once in a while, you just have to go for it. At the AmFam Golf Championship and just had to try to get a selfie with Brett Favre (right). The police officer (background) was actually pretty nice about it.

With Georgia Ellenwood (right), an All-American Track & Field athlete, when she was at the University of Wisconsin.

After a football game at Lambeau Field, I saw two-time US Open Champion Andy North (left) in the parking lot. He was more than happy to take a selfie with me, and so was my buddy Kevin Graff in the background.

*"I don't have the recipe for happiness,
but I think the engine is simply having the desire."*

**Vanessa Paradis,
French model & actress**

The "Happy Zone" Recipe

A **recipe is a set** of instructions for preparing a particular dish, including a list of the ingredients required. It's something that is likely to lead to a particular outcome. In this case, you are not baking a meal, you are putting this together so you will be able to increase your own happiness. The quote above adds a little spice to the recipe. If you have the desire for happiness, you can attain it.

From all of the interviews and research completed, much was learned about what makes people happy. You have hopefully learned ideas to help you on your road to the "happy zone." Remember that the journey is the reward – there is no final destination to your happiness. Here is a list of the most important ingredients needed to attain that "zone." So, get out your mixing bowls, and get ready to prepare your very own "happy zone" recipe.

The first part of the recipe calls to have at least one part gratitude in all things. Be appreciative of what you have while you try to go after all you want. If you can't appreciate what you have, you'll never be as happy as you could be by adding this simple ingredient. This includes giving thanks for gifts you've been given. It also includes using daily life to show kindness to others. Put at least one part gratitude in all you do.

The most important part of attaining happiness is relationships. So, make sure you pour in a lot of relationships in this recipe. This includes family and friends, co-workers, neighbors, and even people you don't know. Do whatever you can to maintain your relationships and nurture them, no matter how far away the people may be. Be kind in the face of adversity and you'll see your happiness skyrocket. You'll have much less frustration and way more happiness in your life.

Part of this recipe will also include rolling up our comparisons. Roll up comparing yourself to others and throw it in the trash. There is no room in this recipe for comparisons. That being said, if you want to strive to be a better person, a happier person, or a healthier person, and you know somebody who is doing a better job than you are at the present time, try to treat life similarly to that person. Don't compare your situation to what is going on in others' lives. Remember, you are not better than anybody else, and nobody else is better than you. We're all in this game of life together.

You'll definitely want to sprinkle in some smiles in this recipe. When you smile, it's very hard to not be in a happy mood. When you start to have negativity enter your life, put on your permanent smile and you'll feel much better. If you have somebody that may be getting on your last nerve, flash a smile. You'll probably both laugh.

Spread in consistency in all areas of your life. Be consistent with your health – eat right and get enough sleep on a regular basis. Put away some money in savings each time you get paid. Pray on a regular basis. Show up on time for work.

Toss in a few cups of sharing in your recipe. Share the gifts you've been given with others. It could be as simple as sharing your time. Give what you can to those who may be in need. What are you good at that may help others? Can you volunteer your time to a cause you find worthy? There are so many options for what you can do. You could be a mentor to a younger person. You could help out a co-worker who may be struggling with a project or assignment. Helping your child with homework is a great way to be more connected to them. You may know a neighbor who is having a tough time with something that has happened to them – maybe you can help out in some way.

You'll need at least one pound of involvement. Be involved in everything you do. Really involved. Be present. Whatever you are doing, concentrate on that task. Don't worry about what you might have to do in the future; this takes away from the present moment. You can't be in the "happy zone" if you are not living in the present.

Whisk in a little bit of help when you need it, and don't be afraid to ask for it. You might be really good with your money, but not so good with your health, or it may be just the opposite. Seek out somebody who is good at what you want to be good at and have them guide you. Maybe you will seek out a co-worker who is really good at something you may be struggling with at work. You might know a neighbor who is a jack-of-all-trades while you can't do anything around the house, and you can ask that person for help. Don't get overly frustrated by what you can't do. Concentrate on what you can do. Frustration will only lead to less happiness.

Throw in a couple spoonfuls of simple. Make it simple on yourself in whatever you are trying to do. Trying to save money? Set up automatic deposits. The same goes for your monthly payments – set them up to be paid automatically. This way you'll have more time for the things you want to do rather than spending time paying bills. Make time for the important stuff. Most of the time it's the simple things in life that end up being the most important. When you look back on the things that make you the happiest, you'll see it's the little things that really did it. Simply being with your family and friends and enjoying their company, watching your kids succeed in their activities, enjoying your hobbies with others – these are all part of what is important.

You will need quite a few sprinkles of listening. Listen to what your body is telling you when it concerns your health and wellness. Listen to what your children are trying to tell you. Listen to your religious leaders. Listen to your boss when he or she gives constructive criticism. Listen to your financial advisor.

A few bagfuls of "now" will help your recipe reach its full potential. Don't wait for the perfect time to start that project. There will never be a perfect time. However, now is the best time. Now is the time to call the friend you haven't seen in a while and schedule a get-together. Now is the time to ask the girl out on a date. Now is the time to learn that skill you've been looking to master. Now is the time to start eating better. Now is the time to have faith. Now is the time to start saving for the future. Now is the time to start the side business you've been waiting on until the right time. Now is the time to stop procrastinating on whatever it is you are looking to do. Now is the time to be happy.

*"Very little is needed to make a happy life;
it is all within yourself, in your way of thinking."*

Marcus Aurelius the Philosopher

About the Author

A graduate of the University of Wisconsin-Platteville, Steve Gehrmann began his career after college as a radio announcer and advertising account executive. He helped area merchants with advertising that helped increase their sales and bottom lines. Along with his advertising duties, he also was the voice of local sports and host of a radio show for a couple of years, discussing everything for listeners, including politics, sports, and local events.

After being in radio for almost ten years, he moved into a career as a certified credit counselor, helping clients reorganize their debts to afford their monthly obligations and get a better handle on their financial futures. He then took on the challenge of working at a mortgage company as a loan counselor and loss mitigation specialist, assisting homeowners who had fallen behind on mortgage payments.

Currently, he helps customers live out their dreams with loans to improve their lives and financial situations.

His entire career has been devoted to helping people achieve better lives, and now with his book, *The Happy Zone*, he has the hope to help as many others as possible to live a happy life.

When at work, he can always be seen with his "happy socks" on – literally – and trying his best to make it 75 and sunny for everybody around him.

He is a devoted husband and father. He also enjoys running with his neighbors, playing poker with his poker club, working out, and watching his favorite sports teams.

MEDIA REQUESTS:
gehrsports@hotmail.com

PRESENTATION & BULK SALE INQUIRIES:
gehrsports@hotmail.com